Bodies of Water
& Women

Made in the USA
2020

Cover Illustration by: Miranda Lorikeet
Book Design by: Kira Gresoski
Editing by: Kallie Falandays
Based on Vintage Book Template by: David Haden

ISBN: 978-1-09833-042-2

www.kiragresoski.com
Kira Gresoski is a love poet. She lives in St. Louis, Missouri.

Printed by BookBaby

Bodies of Water & Women

POEMS & STORIES
KIRA GRESOSKI

For the village of women that raised me

and the Earth, our 4-billion-year-old home

Table of Contents

Chapter One

Chapter Two

Chapter Three

Chapter One

Swimming in Secret Lake

Does it go on forever?

My heartbeat ripples
in the water.
The great blue heron
glides across the sky,
its elegant legs breaking
the lake's glass surface.

The sun, a citrus twist,
shines on my salt lick skin,
my tired limbs like the fins
of some common minnow.

This must be forever,

eternity as a bowl of water
suspended between
the dusky sunset sky
where planets of dust and ice
spin on their spines,
and the sinking miles
where cold-blooded creatures
dwell in the shadows,
and I kick my legs like a duck,
soaking up clouds and colors,
caught in the middle.

I'm skimming across this tension,
an arrow slung through silk,
soft and strong as the element
that first held me
when I was called
out of the darkness
into my mother's body,

when I was called
out of the depths
into my body

Flood Babies

I was born in the flood of '93 into a city,
into a home that was barely floating.

I had to go
fall in love with a man
born and raised on the flood plain,
destined to find our common ground
in the pattern of disaster.

I want us to be the kind of people
who know when to let go,
but when you've carried your life in boxes
up the washed-out basement steps,
or seen your front yard swallowed in the river's belly,
an egret perched on your dad's submerged
International Harvester, your arms may take the shape
of holding on. Sometimes, we hold too much.

I tell the man I love, *don't look at me*
like that. Like what? Like I'm your field of crops
and you're wondering if I'm going to make it.
Not to spoil the ending, but, my darling, we aren't
going to make it, everything we create and grow
and build will be taken. The water always wins.

If we get to take any miracle with us,
it's this:

our eyes are made
mostly of water

and when you look at me
without fear of the future,
with nothing but love
for our tenuous existence,

the worries and clouds
in your knotted brow clear

and the pool in your eyes
reflects the light in mine.

Nightmare of Swimming in Ditches

It's a sewage river, a suburb gutter,
a thread of muddy water weaving
along the thoroughfares and highways.

My mate and I swim through it, paddling
like muskrats with our noses perched
above the murky soup, stirring our paws
beneath the water. We paddle past dead
dishwashers, gutted refrigerators, barrels
of unlabeled chemicals. Whatever

the city doesn't want, it tosses here.
So we pretend this is a jungle stream,
imagine an oasis up ahead,
sacred serpents, lush birdsong and not
the honk and blare of rush hour traffic.

Then, we're at home with showered skin.
There's a knock at the door and a SWAT team
in our yard. They break in before I let them.

A man with a high-tech vacuum
strapped to his chest tells me,
We have to look for something,
but we can't tell you what it is.
A crew waves wands over our furniture,
a woman with a caked face grabs my hand
and pricks it, drawing my blood into a vial.
Just testing for something, she says,
grinning as she does it again.
If I guess what it is you're looking for,
will you tell me if I'm right?
I ask the vacuuming man.
He nods. *You're looking for the atomic waste.*
The waste they dumped in the water, in the ditch.

He nods again, their machines whirring,
beginning to beep. I feel myself sink.

The poison is invisible and everywhere.
And all my life, I've been swimming in it.

My Hometown Is a Trash Fire

Women in my hometown
are trying to make it out with Tupperware
parties, weight loss and hair growth vitamins,
and Mary Kay.

I don't accept the Facebook invites.
When a high school enemy's little sister,
a shy girl who never spoke to me,
sends me a message eight years after graduation

to tell me about her exciting offer, I say
I don't really wear make-up.
Okay, but skin care, she replies,
and I log off.

People in this town are suckers for
one-way carts to the shooting stars,
schemes of being your own boss. For the men,

it's usually meth or a heavy metal band
or poems about God at the open mic.
They see through the matrix. They know
the world's deepest ways.

This Trash Fire Is My Hometown

Deep within the armpit
of our town, a landfill belches up
chains of smoke and when they unfurl
in the wind, they carry

flecks of radioactive waste
all throughout our village. West Lake
Landfill is an unmarked burial ground
for the atom bomb, runoff from

Mallinckrodt's uranium production
decaying into a cancer cocktail.
I pour myself a drink
and watch the documentary where my neighbors

slowly die: a teenage son
with Stage 4 lymphoma, his mom quitting
her job so she can give care fulltime,
guiding him toward a dignified death.

A grandma lived near the landfill
for thirty years, tending the backyard
garden each season, canning the fruits
of her labor into sauces and jams,

with no idea the amount of hazardous
waste in her dirt was two hundred times
the EPA's safe limits. She thought
she was giving her grandchildren the gift of love

and homemade tomato sauce, not feeding them
the history of all the people
we once destroyed in an instant,
now haunting our bloodline

for generations. I'm aching
for every kid born here with a dream
of breaking out, scaling pyramids to the top.
I'm angry, but not surprised,

to find the atom bomb aftermath
was dumped in secret. No one knew
it was there until the stench of rotten eggs
punctuated the morning traffic.

Republic Services, owner of the landfill,
says the waste is contained,
even as an underground trash fire licks
its forked tongue to the source of sickness.

Our Home Is On Fire

This is my home: our trash is on fire,
our air smells sour,
and our water remembers
the day we split the sky.

I love the people who live here,
and if my pockets were deep enough,
I'd buy all the make-up and Tupperware
needed to give us a clean way out.

I've always thought we were more
than just hardscrabble fighters,
down-on-their-luck hustlers, barely-scraping-buyers,
always thought there was something superhuman
in our ability to forge a life against the slow burn
death of apathy and industry.

I'm proud to be from these people,
commoners with a rare kind of love,
call it contagious, call it radioactive,
call it inhaling all the dead at once.

Family of Origin Stories

I was the daughter of a Marlboro dragon. This was not
our home planet. Money was bad and so were the people
who sold their souls to have it (we didn't have it).

At six years old, I fell asleep crying to Animal Farm.
Someone was always reading me a story, or ranting and raving
or singing and spinning a yarn.
The world was ending before my life began,
and my family sighed *oh well.*
Humanity is ugly anyway. A cruelty we can't understand.
Better to be a cat or a tree or a dead star in the sky.
Nothing and no one out there could be trusted,
but love was why we tried to survive.

Every time we said goodbye, we said *I love you.*
I love you meant *don't die.*

Mama Bear Is a Dancing Bear

Mama Bear is a bear in the circus, wearing
a tutu. Mama Bear cries at every commercial
of animal abuse. When Mama Bear was a girl,
she grew up in a townhome she can still see
through the kitchen window in the townhome where she
watered and raised her two love-cubs. When she was young,
the stories say she was unstoppable, a blur of whirling motion.
Couldn't fall asleep until she thrashed her legs against the bed
and wore herself out, running marathons in her dreams.

When I'm sixteen, she asks me to watch her dance routine
in the basement, confessing she believes in past lives,
and in hers, she was a ballerina.
She leaps and twirls and floats light-footed
among clear plastic totes of her dead grandma's clothes,
which she can't let go, and a litter box filled
with cascading envelopes, medical bills and credit card statements
and whatever else is trying to kill
Mama Bear's wild spirit. I believe her when she dances,
believe this is an art she's practiced lifetimes, and I feel she's trying
to tell me something, something about animals in cages
or souls inside bodies or how we survive our own lives,
how we carve into the river of time when we move
to loud music, drowning out the world's sorrows.

Mama Bear lets me borrow her black dresses
that shimmer like waters of rayon and silk,
and they fit me like a dream, so I can't let them go.
In the days when I feel the weight of a planet bearing
on my neck, I remember Mama Bear shaking herself free
and I make the space to dance.

Picture of Snow at Seven Years Old

Outside, the rutted roads fill with snow,
pines shake dander from their boughs.
Inside our school, paper snowflakes
dangle from the ceiling by threads.

In art class, we're tasked with drawing a winter night:
a lone snowman on his hill, in a sea of stars.
We're given rough sheets of black paper, a bucket
of ancient crayons, wrappers unraveling from waxy bodies.
Silence drifts over us.

When we're done, we line up to show Ms. Sharon our pictures.
You all drew white snow, she snaps, my paper in her hand,
but if you would actually look closely, (she's always accusing us
of not looking closely)
snow isn't just white, it's also blue.

Ms. Sharon was never happy with what we made her.
She'd rather have a cabin in Montauk, an icy river to walk alone,
nowhere to be but her easel, than to be here with us,
our blue-black eyes and unbrushed hair, our outbursts of anger,
and this artless town nestled under the blanket
of poverty and piss-yellow snow.

All I wanted was a gold star for everything I did,
but what she taught me I've taken into every winter night.
I wasn't going to get applauded for drawing a pretty little picture.
I had to forget the image I'd been sold and see everything fresh,
for the first time. On the drive home, I stared out
the window, and I couldn't believe I'd never seen it.

The snow was shining the sky across its surface.
It was blue. It covered everything I loved.

Something in the Water

There's something strange
in my family's blood.

Our snakes of DNA
swallow their own tails,
weaving a trail of bad luck.

Does it all begin with the creek
where I used to lead the herd of boy-cousins,
gathering fleets of maple leaves
and shipping them down the chugging gulley
as the rain beat its gentle fists into the mud?

What is it about Cold Water Creek
that circles around our geographies,
our memories?

We've splashed in the humble waters of the creek
for generations, first my father, then me,
and now this: my brother born with a birth defect,
rare as one in 100,000, my other brother
born dead, cleft lip, shriveled leg,
heart on the outside of his body.

When I go searching for answers,
one report insists we lay our questions to rest.
The author claims there isn't enough radioactive waste
in the water to take the blame, not enough research
to declare the red flares of rare illnesses on a map of the creek
are connected in a cancer cluster.

They suggest the worst part
of living near radioactivity is that the constant fear
and dread will make you sick.

What they know for certain is this:

we're dying,
not because our water carries the legacy of war,
but we because we live in this part of town,
because we're poor.

Choosing a Tombstone

The mausoleum where my little brother's ashes
sleep is the nicest room our family has ever known.
Our grief echoes off the white marble and the bowls
of running water make our keening sound musical.

Not traditionally religious, my parents chose a bronze urn
of Mary and Jesus, the son bloody and brutalized, cradled again
in his earth mother's lap, maybe as a reckoning with
whatever God or Natural Hand placed their son's heart
on the outside of his body.

My other little brother, alive as a tornado at my side,
peeks into the glass at the loin-clothed figure and asks,
Tarzan? We fill the cool corridors of death with laughter,
the snot swinging from my dad's nose in a vine.

Before and after this day, Dad sticks to his plan. *Don't waste
your money, just take me to the ocean and dump me over
the side of the boat.* Mom wants her ashes scattered on
the dry fields of her grandma's farmhouse in Belmont,
Mississippi, and a small piece of her here, in a vase
with her favorite child.

At seven years old, I may be the only one of my kin
who wants to choose herself a tombstone, a slab of granite,
a rock plaque to proclaim something like,
She remembered everything, or
Her heart tried to be both: water and earth.

Now I know it's possible to be buried
in a seed pod that gives birth to a tree, the roots feeding
from the fetal-positioned body, but I didn't know it that day
as I stepped out of the brisk tomb into the blazing sun
and emerald, manicured lawn.

Above the rows and rows of stones,
the evenly spaced trees stood sentinel,
outstretched arms waving at us and the sky,
declaring in total silence what I would spend
my whole life trying to shout.

Sisterhood in the Wild, Sisterhood as Biological Adaptation

A feral tangle of hair & limbs & hunger,
I was more wolf pup than girl child
when friends taught me the art
of feminine armor—eyebrows tweezed
& sleeked into daggers, eyelids painted iridescent,
like the scales of a venomous fish.

My family called my untamed mane
a rat's nest, but sisters took my hair
into their hands,

teaching me to braid, gathering
the strands into triplet rivers,
keeping wild in place with a pin.

Together we learned: a girl can never
have too much protection, so travel
in cackling packs, make each other laugh like hyenas,
throw your head back & boast your fangs.

If it's time to part ways,
walk the other girl halfway, for safety.

If a man drives his car in circles
around you both, touching himself,
his earthworm nakedness in broad day,
remember Discovery Channel & what to do
if you're alone in the woods with a bear.

If you have a stick, shake it in his face.

If you have an ax, chop him into wood
& light a fire so you & your sisters
can dance in circles around the flames.

If all you have is your voice, then run.

Make it home, tell her mom, lock the doors.
Slither next to your sister, chameleon into the couch.

Drudge up memories like
the remains of daughters
drowned in lakes:
a neighbor who asked if you
would dance for him in the grass,
a softball coach who whispered in her ear
when she made it home safe.

Push the stories back to the mucky bottom,
past the shadows and human-sized catfish.

Then do what your girls do best:
make your own fun & mind your own business.

Open your sister's fridge
as if it is your fridge,

and make yourself the sandwich of the summer.
Salami and swiss. Rye bread. Butter lettuce.
Pickles from her mom's garden. Pop open a bag
of ruffled chips, eat until you swell.
Suck the cheese dust from your fingers
like butterflies guzzling nectar.

Drape your legs across each other,
dream about the future,
invent the world that should exist.

Radio Girl Is Born

A baby no one wants ends up in a dumpster.

It happens every day.

This time, no one hears her cries.

This time, she doesn't die.

Call it miracle, call it science fiction,
but she survives the chuck into a garbage truck,
the tumble of trash onto a landfill mountain.

She arrives at the site of a strange power.

This landfill's stuffed with radioactive runoff.
The aftermath of the atom bomb is a kind of karma.

Uranium and radon bubble and burp
through a crack in the earth,
rearranging her DNA.

She isn't like us. Doesn't need mother's milk.
She's sustained by the waste.

She learns to read with our trashed wrappers
and receipts. She learns who humans are
by what we discard.

New messages arrive every day, the dinosaur trucks
hurtling away, their bodies groaning.

Her body, like the earth, can hold tremendous pain
under its skin. Her cells take in what's toxic
and give her the strength to live.

Chapter Two

The Path to Secret Lake

We learned our way to Secret Lake
from the college kids who came before us, the ones
who drove Michigan Ave. until it becomes gravel,
until the gravel gives way to woods,
and past the fortress of trees, you can glimpse
a glimmer of water. It's a hand-me-down secret
so we keep it to ourselves, the way we weave
the narrow path, crownvetch and thistle biting
at our ankles, gnats and mosquitos buzzing in the air
thick as Southern speech.

Heirs to the dirt path, we never look back
and swim on the sandy public beaches
where frat boys chug sun-warmed rum
and moms slap sunscreen on their kids' skin.

Our face of the lake is different,
curving around thicketed hills into the sunset.
Our beach is a patch of dirt and grass,
stones tumbling down to weedy water.

Our lake is filled with a mud
that sucks your toes like a deranged lover.

Secret Lake is the place where we practice
the art of becoming invisible, growing so still
the fish flash their scales in the sun
all around us. If you wanted us to trade our little lake
for a five-star vacation, we wouldn't bite.
We'd tell you about swimming in the lake at night,
our flashlights bobbing down the shadowy path
as we break free from the trees into the black velvet sky
spilling its riches, the dazzling light of infinite stars
which we bless with our wishes, like coins tossed in a fountain.

You can keep your crowds, your loud shutter
of a thousand cameras pointed in the same destination's direction.
We'll take the lake and make ourselves disappear inside it.

Radio Girl Studies the Mushroom

On the outskirts of town, where deer forge
trails into the thicket, mushrooms pop up
red and round as buttons, brown and soft as suede,
all sizes and shades of velvet umbrellas.

Some are deadly, some edible, all do holy work.
Radio Girl kneels to the damp earth, puts her ear
to the leaf-litter quilt, and listens
to the mushrooms sending their mycelium tendrils
into the depths of dirt. Their networks spread miles
in a dense web of threads that collect death,
turning it to fertile soil. Oil spills, heavy metals,
radioactive debris—mushrooms will eat their way
through anything, drawing the damage into their bodies.

Radio Girl puts a hand to her belly
and forgives herself for always being hungry.

She absorbs herself in studying this energy,
this ability to transform toxicity
into tenderness, their delicate bodies teaching her
the wisdom of digging deep into the ground.

Cleaning as Therapy for Women Who Can't Afford It

We're not just getting the grime and rust.
We're on our hands and knees, scrubbing

at the stain of everyone who's ever touched us
just to feel the heat in themselves. We buff

the memories of dead, cold fathers, and leather
belts, red welts, scrub at the cinema starlet's dream

of true love versus the way our lives turned out.
We dig our fists and wrists into the grout.

We polish the floors until they gleam,
until they shine so well we can see ourselves.

Bedtime at Grandma Nightingale's

We had to bathe until we scrubbed the world off us.
Grandma sniffed our hair
to be sure we washed it.
She sent us back and shampooed our scalps herself
if we hadn't. Only once we were clean as the day
we were born could we climb
into her bed and nestle into her starched field of linen.
Before we drifted into our dreams of dinosaurs
and apocalypse, Grandma kneeled beside us
praying, *If I should die before I wake,*
I pray the Lord my soul to take.
Then, with watery eyes, she'd say, *I'd die for you, I'd jump*
in front of a bullet. If you died, my life would be nothing.

I didn't like praying.
I didn't like the look in the eyes of a person
who didn't live for their own sake.
Still, I'll take what she gave me with all I've had to unlearn.
That woman full of worry taught me everything
I know about making a room beautiful.
In the temple of her quiet home, I felt the world
couldn't touch me. I was a royal heir,
or a bear cub, blanketed in fur in an earthen den,
the lamp light on the wall making
a gold moon, and her reading
us a story about a lost little puppy,
who wandered off from the others
following all the wrong things,
and how he was now slowly,
but surely,
making his way home.

I Only Want to Play Outside

I know
it's lucky
to be put on a shelf
like a porcelain doll,
to be begged not to break,
but I was not a weak child.
At home, I ran wild with a pack
of feral kids and I was the leader,
the dreamer of stories and adventures.
Until my brother died and I was told to
play inside, watch TV, not leave the house.

Witchcraft for Neurotic Women

Place seven stones in a perfect circle. One for justice,
one for peace, five more to know the difference
and hold in your fist. Light candles
with color-coded intentions. Clean every corner
of your house. Don't do magic when there's dishes
in the sink or you'll attract more dirty dishes. Don't manifest
when there's filthy thoughts in your mind or you'll call in
more chaos. Tiger's eye for balance and harmony, a wand
of rose quartz to sweep out the trauma cobwebs from your pussy,
obsidian crystal balls for shadow-work, moving through darkness
toward the light, and amethyst for answering emails.
Touch gems to your temples before you fall asleep each night.

Chunks of salt around the door, bundles of sage strung
along the windows, protect every possible entrance.

The moon will be at its fullest at 10:53 p.m., rearrange your plans
so you can be front row as the orb-eye reaches the pinnacle of light.
Leave jars full of water in the center of the garden to absorb
cosmic power. Say the same thing to yourself a hundred times a day.
You are growing. You are brilliant, beautiful. You are safe.
Gather basil, thyme, and ginger into a jar to bring you money
and fill it with honey. Shake the jar every time the poor old thoughts
come in and repeat, *I am a rich, rich witch. I am rich.*
Money loves me, and I love money. Bring the jar to the bank.
Shake it in the face of a banker. Take out your life savings.
Buy a broomstick. A plane ticket. Take everything
that ever hurt you and burn it one minute after midnight. Fly away.

Answering the St. Louis Question

They ask you where you went to high school
but they really want to know:

How much money does your family make?
How much violence did you see in your home?

Did your school lose accreditation?
Or did it have full-ride scholarships
for everyone who graduated?

Do you have a network, connections?
Or do your connections form a cycle and chain that won't break?

To all their nosey ass questions, I give a single answer:
I'm from North County, bitch

Everything I needed to learn,
I learned in North County

In North County, you learn to drive slow
so you don't hit the herds of kids
who wander right through
the middle of the streets

You learn to eat the fast food
your mama brings your grateful asses
after work and before her night classes,
with ravenous gratitude
in front of the TV,
shoveling it in mindlessly,
you drop some ketchup on your knee,
you scoop that shit up with a French fry

You learn kids have such a need to claim a side

so we've got kids with rat tails and buzz cuts waving
confederate flags from their trucks, the stars of team genocide
inked onto their sunken chests with pride, kids with a long bus ride
from the city every morning,
sent to detention and disciplinary meetings
for coloring coding their clothing
with histories of loyalty, family, war, and royalty,
and a random group of mostly white dudes,
who, whenever they see each other,
bend their knees, angle their elbows, spread their wings
and caw to each other across the hallways,
who call themselves *The Crows*

We've got average Midwesterners
acting like they're already Kardashian Famous.
White girls get wasted, belt Kanye lyrics in a ranch home basement

In North County you learn womanhood from messy girls,
sisterhood from girls at war with their mothers

Sacrifice and strength from seventeen year olds,
stamina from Melissa who goes to work
right after school every single day
so she can help her immigrant parents pay their bills

She celebrates herself every moment of her life,
and on her rare day off, gets you high,
feeds you a feast, plays you all her favorite songs

You could write a song about learning to kiss
with Marie after the party, because vodka
turns you into a sloppy puppy the first time
you're drunk, all wiggle and tongue. You will be taught
softness by people who have lived such harsh lives

Learn how to hold someone when their mother dies
or goes back to jail or drugs or loses custody
of their younger siblings or when their father commits
suicide. And they find him

You learn to let people grieve at an arm's length,
when they don't want to be held,
just poured a drink,
or passed the pipe,
or let into the circle,
even when they feel so empty
they have no stories to tell

North County teaches you that dissatisfaction tastes
like 95% of students getting free and reduced lunches,
hunching through the lunch line, packed body to body,
hungry for the spicy chicken, before they finally get
to sit down in the divided cafeteria
and scarf that shit down in six quick minutes

But bliss? Bliss tastes like field day,
a party packed body to body on the blacktop,
dancing and chanting and swaying,
as you say what we can only say with body language:
you are here and I am here and so
we move together,

when a fight breaks out,
and one person starts running
toward the scene, and soon everyone
is swept into a human stampede,
and you and hundreds of other kids
are pounding the pavement like an ocean tide,
and it's not just because you want to see the fight,
which will be over by the time you get there and begin again
with the first ring of the bell on Monday morning,

no, it's because you can't resist the pull of belonging,
the unstoppable force of running someplace
as one body

The Scrubs

The sex symbol is sick of being sexy,
the rock star wants to slip on
fuzzy pajamas, take an Ambien, pass out,
just the same as your mom on the couch
after her overnight shift as an ER nurse,
because everyone's tired.
The planet and its people are tired,
because it's exhausting taking vitals,
checking patients and topping charts,
cranking out another hit single, another
cup of pills, just like it's exhausting
to save lives, to give people a reason
for being alive. It's hard work,
these sold-out stadiums, these maxed-out
hospitals and prisons, these stores
of panicked people, these unruly
mobs of people, these endless wanting, needy
people, and you get worn down, just trying
to find out exactly what your job is
within it. Sometimes you want to slip it off
completely, the meaning of your own life,
the burden of being this fabulous, this
useful and beautiful.

The Stars

You love the music too much to quit it,
no matter how hectic it gets, no matter
the soundtrack sounds less like bass lines
and beat drops when the EKG machine
flatlines, no matter how loud the blood pounds
when a star, who flew too close to the music,
locked himself in a hotel room, swallowed
all the bottles, turned himself blue,
is wheeled into your ward full of people
who will never be ready to die. In your line of work,
it's always showtime. You can't rehearse this.
Just a day in the life. Still, you're tasked
with bringing him back, or the stage
goes black and silent.

The Magic of Make-Up for Melodramatic Teen Girls

When we first made-up each other's faces,
we didn't try to make it beautiful.
We weren't mimicking the models
selling watches and blood diamonds
in the waterlogged magazines
stashed by the toilet,
their white faces painted
to look as plain and pore-less
as a Midwest prairie.

Nope. We turned each other into clowns.
We dabbled in abstract expressionism.
We felt more natural in glam and drag
than competing for Miss Missouri,

with our crimson and violet lipstick
circling all the way out to our chins,
big, thick eyebrows caked-on like caterpillars,
goatees and mustaches, gummy blue eyelids.
Warts and scars and glitter.

We took pictures, doubled over,
laughter knotting ribbons up our ribs.
We cackled in the mirror
at our own delicious wickedness.
Who could be the strangest, the funniest?
She would be our queen, no contest.

Health & Wellness for Obsessive Women

Eat a healthy diet of fiber and air. Compare
yourself to the measuring tape at the starlet's waist,
hire her personal trainer. Share pictures of your flab-before
and fit-after, log and blog your quest for perfection.

Or don't. Don't feed a trillion-dollar industry's idea of beauty
before you feed your own body what it longs for,
what it needs. You can move because it feels good to move,
sweat because it gives you pleasure to glisten in the sun,
rest because you relish the breath
that rises and falls.

You can eat the rainbow. You can eat whatever leaves you full.

The Boys Say You Can't Trust Something That Bleeds

for seven days without dying.

The four-point buck they shot through the heart
while their fathers watched proudly from the tree-stand?

The boys can trust this.

The video game citizens, zombies, and monsters
they conquer in a hailstorm of bullets, the game controllers
vibrating with each kill in their hands and laps?

The boys can trust that.

But girls slipping tampons and pads from their purses,
getting passes to see the nurse, braiding each other's hair
and cradling each other's heads in their laps, scowling with hands
clasped in prayer over the paunch of their soft bellies?

Something's up with that.

With all the blood we leave in the drain, in the dirt,
the way we move among the living, trailing the smell
of wet iron pipes and rust, the boys can't trust us.

They can't understand how we're still standing,
why we didn't die a long time ago.

The Only Girl in a Car Full of Boys

What did I love about being the only girl
in a car full of boys?
I loved the way Marky's rusted red Honda Civic
felt like a spaceship, and how I felt
huddled inside it, sitting in the bitch seat,
smooshed between the boulders of their bodies,
safe in the smell of their cigarette smoke
and cheap aftershave for beards
they couldn't grow. I loved the way
the music crushed us, the bass of blown-out speakers
slamming into our young animal bodies,
the way we drove in a bubble of loud sound
toward trouble. Like a moth getting high
on the zap of a porch light, we were hungry
for anything that might make us burst.
When Marky made a sharp turn, we all yelled
Corners! and dog-piled onto whoever was
sitting on that side of the car. When we drove
over the river, I stood outside the moon roof
and unleashed all the ache in my lungs. Knees
knocking knees. A song about hopping in puddles.
I was happy to be the strange girl or the butt
of their jokes, the cruelest boy handing me
his pack of smokes. *Pack my cigarettes. Look,
she's actually packing my cigarettes!*

Why did I love this?
Was it as simple as the false sense of safety
and closeness, the way we nestled
into each other's scent?

What I didn't love is when they didn't listen.
One night someone spotted a possum in the street
and Marky sped up to hit it.

I yelled for him to stop but he didn't.
He barreled over the possum once
and with the lift of the wheels
I could feel in my stomach,
he threw his car in reverse and drove over
the creature again.
The boys cheered.
Someone yelled it wasn't dead yet
so then Marky, son of a pastor,
the first boy to say he loved me like a sister,
which is when I knew I was still searching
for my missing brother in every car full of boys
and cavernous-damp basement room,
popped his trunk, took out a baseball bat,
and finished what he started.
The boys took turns. Taylor, the first boy
I swore I loved, who I wrote sad songs for,
who touched me in the basement when his friends
weren't far off, persisting when I pushed his hands off,
wore a look of pure delight as he beat the life out
of what was already dead.

They piled back in,
faces flushed,
happily panting like a litter of puppies.

Take me home, I said, my anger a glacier
in my throat. If my voice didn't stop them
from doing what they were always going to do,
I would turn the car to ice, suck all the joy
from the room. They tried to explain why
they did it: because possums are evil, varmint,
cat-killers. They were just being good little
neighborhood pest control, good little vigilante soldiers.
But what did the boys know
about the private lives of unloved creatures?
Why couldn't they stop

to imagine the possum's happiness

as she found a half-eaten apple at the top
of the trashcan, or ask if she had her own joeys
waiting for her in their nest, who found comfort
in the warmth of her fur, who hitched a ride
on her shoulders, who now waited in the dark
for her to return and give them what they wanted

Mush of Water and Bread

Mama is always finding small, sick animals.
A raccoon struck in the street,
a squirrel with a broken leg, a baby bird fallen
from the maple in our backyard.
Like the others, she nestles it in a washrag,
cradles it in a shoebox, steals it to our basement.
Teaching me the art of the eyedropper, one finger
on the trigger, sucking in the soggy mixture,
a mush of water and bread, she says *this is how
you give. Just drip-drop at a time,* and the bird
rises to fullness on two crooked wings.

One spring, a bunny is brought in, abandoned
by its mother. In the shoebox, the velvet infant
quakes with seizure, twitching and tearing
itself apart at the seams, wet black eyes pointed
in a direction I've never seen, and Mama tells me
not to look. Alone, she crouches into the last
spasms of pain, cooing and hushing the creature,
her voice a lullaby. I never knew why
she thought the animals might die easier inside.

But then, I was just a child. I didn't know
what women know about waking up in a pool of blood
in the middle of the night, or trips to the clinic,
where you make the choice to save your own life,
and I couldn't imagine that it was easier for Mama to cry
over the fate of a furred or feathered creature,
than it was for her to cry over us, her babies
that suffered earthside and her babies that died
inside her, their final kicks snapping
within the swell of her skin.

The Waitress on Her Period

It's Easter Sunday and at high noon, the blood
of the moon gushes between my legs,
clotting my cotton pad
in marmalade chunks.
I butter my arms with piping hot plates,
and carry three water glasses in just two hands—
the father, the son, and the holy refill.

Lusting for the cook whose sweat salts the food,
I yell at him through the steaming window
in search of my table's missing toast,
and he screams back, sharpening
his eyes against mine, though when
I slide him a glass of water,
he calls me his wife and melts.

He botches an order and sends out
a clattering plate. Through the din he coos,
For my little cockroaches!
and the waitresses swarm
our first bites all day,
a dish of biscuits and gravy, forks stabbing,
wolves at a fresh kill.

When the rushing crowd dies to a trickle,
I can finally slip to the bathroom,
shedding the apron stuffed with wads
of syrup-sticky cash,
and unroll my sweat-sealed pants.
I gaze
into the face of the miracle of life.
It smells like the kitchen sink,

full of food and rusting, a spout that drains despair

away from me, an iron river:
I know where we come from. I know why we're here.
The blood sings,
I continue to serve. When asked,
I button back the sleeves of the quiet man at A3,

his arm slack from a stroke. I crush his oyster crackers
in their package and rip open the seam
so he can sprinkle them into
the warm pool of his soup,
which I've ladled, spoonful by spoonful,
into the chipped bowl filled to the brim,

then washed clean so many times
I've lost count.

Portrait of a Dying Man With a Jar of Pickles

Love, like all the things I know to do with my hands,
is an art of careful layering. Like making a sandwich.
Or fetching my Papa a Claussen pickle when he's dying
of cancer on hospice care in the living room. Even though
he's stopped talking, and the words he once spoke have
migrated to his eyes, (which burn so brightly they startle me
more than the bones that dig like spoons through his skin)
he still craves that electric shock: of sour, seed, and crunch.
First, he flaps his hands and hums to let us know he's wanting.
Then, he raises a bony finger and points to the Claussen
I'm eating. His mouth ajar like a baby bird's, Grandma mists his
throat with a spray bottle to help him swallow. *This was his idea,*
she boasts, bragging about the genius of his mind the way he would.
She waters the mouth she's kissed a lifetime the way she would
a houseplant. Nothing left to do in marriage but become the rain,
that eternal nurse. I relish this last layer of love, prying the jar
open. I untwist the puckered lid that pops like the valve of a heart
and bring him a dying wish, the briny flesh bursting into a green
vinegar river down his chin, his eyelids fluttering shut.

The Blood Stitch

The heart is a bitch who knits.
She's a patient woman. Child
after grandchild, stitch after stitch.
When I fall asleep, my blood and breath
make a blanket, as a wise woman
sits in my chest and clicks her wrists,
her needles clinking, ringing a bell of steady
metal sound—the best art is repetition. The best art
is a gold throw blanket my grandma crocheted for me,
each row of stitches knotted with precision,
a secretary's impeccable print. The mind gets all
the credit. The brain is boss in his grey labyrinth
of rooms, perched on his white column throne of bone.
The heart is meat and ache and thankless work.

The mind forgets
it's not the only one with a message.
My grandpa was a mailman. Believed he was a prophet,
a livewire straight to God. Beside every man in the light
of divine fire, there's a wife, writing in the margins,
tracking the budget, counting the losses. The heart has a mind
of its own, wringing out problems and prayers with each beat,
and the mind would do well to go quiet and listen to her speak.
A textbook Scorpio, Papa's stories are the ones we'll tell
for generations, while my grandma, whose name I couldn't say
as a baby, and so I called her Moo, my Grandma Moo
is a Taurus through and through. Persistent as a bull,
steady as the kind-eyed gaze of a cow grazing on daisies,
grass melting on its tongue. The world is a softer place
when I sleep beneath the blankets she's made.
Warmed by this fabric force field, I think of her
and the heart's insistence—that seamstress in my chest.
All my life, my heart knits. And in my blood, I feel a thread.

The Waitress Feeds a Cowboy

The sun bleeds through the sky
   and I let out a sigh as the day
      dies down, the diner windows
washed in a holy pink glow.
   I move slowly between the booths,
      refilling jellies, dusting sugar crumbs
into my palm, pausing for the crooner
   on the stereo singing Blue Velvet.
      Even after endless hours of these empty
moments, my heart still sings along
   to the old-school softness.
      I can feel the blood beat in my damp,
velvet muscles pulsating after eight hours
   on my feet. Throbbing
      with tenderness for all who hunger,
I put my hand on the old man's shoulder
   and say a little prayer for him, our Cowboy Chuck.
      Chuck eats with us seven nights a week.
Always, the same table. Always, a sweet tea
   and a diet plate. He asks about my life,
      trades me tales of who he used to be
in those golden days, the folk hero
   rattling from the war time to the coal mines,
      then packing up his guitar for the traveling show.
He flips open his wallet with his big pickin' thumb
   and shows me a photo of him and his late wife.

His *dead* wife is what I mean. It's more honest.
   But *late* is the soft old way to say it.
      Late makes it seem like a warm dream,
like she was only running late for dinner,
   so now the cowboy holds this table
      for the two of them until eternity.

The Waitress Brings the Cowboy His Bill

I wait on Chuck for years before he lets me down,
years of him buying me breakfast on my days off,
while I ask him questions and listen to him talk.
I hope someone will do this for me
when I'm old someday, if the world isn't just
the fastball of treacherous flame they claim is coming.

If I even get to live to be eighty,
I hope someone will let me pay
for their coffee, eggs, and toast
while I boast of the little I learned
of my time here on Earth,
and I hope they'll still love me
when I'm backwards and wrong.

After many folk songs about his wife,
his happy life, Chuck tells a small bite of a story
about his daughter, then lowers his eyes and sighs,
but she's so fat though, shaking his head with disgust,
his turkey skin warbling under his neck,
even though at seventy-nine he still tries
to make it to the gym three times a week.

So Chuck is a jerk.
So Chuck tips better than any other regular
and actually knows a single detail about my life.
People hardly ever surprise me
in their ability to be multiple things at once.

I spend hours tableside,
looking for the goodness inside, filling their cups
a sip below the brim,
secretly chanting my waitress mantra:

feed and care for everyone,
trust no one to be as sweet as the tea you serve.

I make the tea myself in a witch's boiling pot,
pouring sugar by the pitcher into
the hissing mouth of running water,
and I walk and trot glasses of the good stuff
all day to people who act like they run the place,

but I run this place, I'm the one running,

so I know good and well
even people who drink long and deep
at the well of God's nectar
all have a little rot in their teeth.

No shame there. It's the name of the game.
Everyone at the table thinks
they're the star of the show, the lone hero,
but the waitress knows
they're just another hungry people.
I bring Chuck the check. None of us are here
to have it all figured out, but here
to eat and make our living and pay our rent
and care for each other, even when we're not impressed
with each other, to press our ears and lips open
to exchange this world with one another. *Hi. How can I help you?*
Thank you. Bye. Take care now. Have a good day.

In Love With a Lake

I surrender my rigid inner mind
each time I step foot in the divine
silky liquid of the lake.

My sisters and I slither out
of our swimsuits once the water ripples
up to our chests. We press ourselves
skin-to-skin with the water's wet kiss.

Our voices flit and fill the muggy air
with chitters of joy and sighs and laughter.

Then, without sudden announcement,
but gradually, like the drift of sediment,
a silence settles.

My stinging thoughts go dead nettle.
The only sound is water sloshing
on the weedy, reeded shoreline,
and in the distance,
a solitary hawk,
distant cousin of the dinosaurs,
squawking.
Enough talking.
Swimming in the lake,
our bodies become
listening instruments,

and we are free to be naked,
with nothing to say.

Portrait of Chris's Mom After the Flood

The river was once a distant glint, a snake of sunlight
   on the horizon. Now, we're wading through its belly.
      Chris drives down the highway to his parents' house,

past what was a military march of soy fields and corn stalks.
   All the orderly rows of cash crops are now underwater.
      A deer thrashes through, up to its chest

in the thick of the flood, barely making its way forward, each lunge
   rippling out. We park behind his family's fleet
      of vehicles on the shoulder, fight through the sky

of jubilant mosquitoes to stare at his childhood home,
   rebuilt on stilts because his family's been here before.
      '93 was the last time the water rose this high

and I don't like to wonder what's ahead as the records
   continue to climb. His parents arrive, accepting our offering:
      a paper bag of cheeseburgers and chicken strips.

Chris's mom, who lost most of her family photos
   in a flood, then lost what remained in a house fire, who grew
      in her own inner waters the man I want to love forever,

drapes a threadbare towel over her shoulders like a queen's cloak.
   She takes a folding chair from the hood of her car,
      snaps it open and sinks into its rusted frame.

She surveys the water, the renegade septic tank
   bobbing in her front yard, the manic hum of bugs
      that quench their thirst with our blood,

the washed-out state highway that news crews will drive down
   to get B-roll footage and interviews, microphones shoved in

the faces of folks who haven't slept in seven days.

She takes it all in, this godforsaken kingdom where too much of
the very thing that keeps you alive will kill you.
She looks at me and asks, laughing, *Well,*

you wanna go for a swim?

The Lake Has Secrets

You swim in a lake for two summers and think you really know its every mood and hue. Then, one July day at high noon, you and your friends simmer under a skin-crisping sun, when the sheriff putters toward you in his dinky motorboat. *You guys can't be swimming out here, it isn't safe. This part of the lake is reserved for fishermen and their boats,* he shouts over the engine's whine-and-chop. Nodding and agreeing to leave, you watch him make his way around the bend. *There's no way we aren't going to swim here.* In two years, it's been you and the fishes, the great blue heron and waves of silence, only once or twice a boat on the horizon. No one loves this lake like us, so we won't just give it up. The calm erupts and he's back again. *Now I didn't want to tell you kids this, but the locals all call this place Shit Lake. All the sewage from town gets piped out here, and you really don't want to be in it when there's an E Coli outbreak.* This time, he watches you turn around, swimming back through the water you've baptized yourself in so many times, wondering if you ever knew the lake at all. This body of water you bask in, inspiring your romantic poetry that aches for the sublime, isn't what you think it is, some gift from Mother Earth, carved and watered into her skin from the loving hands of time. One hundred years ago, a bunch of white supremacist, corn-bred, evangelist men sweated in their linen shirts and stiff suits, deciding in a council meeting that the town needed a lake. So, a creek was dammed and trees were razed down to stumps and the earth was drilled open, so the lake could be stocked with fish the men wanted to hook. You think you've discovered a secret piece of utopia, a secret place of peace. You like the idea of being a courageous woman, swimming heart-thrust-forward into the cosmic sunset. But you're up to your neck in the village's shit, the work of men and machines.

A Storyteller Is Born

You cover your brother's ears with your cupped hands.
Your parents' screams rattle the vents, up from the basement
into the room you share, the sounds of lungs tearing.

Some nights, you fall out of bed and press your ear
to the hole in the floor. You're collecting their words.
You're listening hard to make their animal pain into meaning.

But tonight, you shield your little brother and tell him a story.
Something ordinary about queens and castles and gardens.
It's boring because everyone is safe and nothing bad ever happens.

Sissy, this story is so long, he says, sounding sleepy.
You're just letting the story flow, you're hardly here at all. Your voice
pours out of you, warming your body, a steady light in the dark.

Still, their voices claw up the walls. They must not be here at all.
You're determined to match them word for word. The more
they keep you from sleep, the deeper you'll dream a new world.

You're a difficult child. *(Autobiographical poet? Fuck, good luck).*
You were the baby paying attention, watching them in silence, now
as the woman who writes it down.

You could ask for forgiveness. Knowing the pain of shared stories,
you could erase the parts that are uncomfortable, unflattering.
But you need it to be said: in the morning, your parents apologized

for fighting. Said they loved you very much. They were just
fighting over money. You became a storyteller because they read
you books, sang you songs, told you stories.

Even then, you sensed the stream of visions
in your head was a gift and maybe someday you'd use it
to make lots of money.

So far writing pays as much as any job you've had:
enough to live.
But writing makes you rich in something money can never touch.

This art teaches you to see yourself, to exist outside
the life you've been given.
The story teaches you to sit with all your nerves and grit
and need for sleep
and to tell the world *no, this*

this is who I'm going to be.

Radio Girl Listens to the Air Waves

She lies down on a bed of moss
on the far end of town, imagines
she was the kind of girl with four walls,
a bedroom to call hers,
but it's all open-air here, far enough away
from the streetlights to see a sprinkling
of stars beyond the grasping fingers
of the trees. Like any lonely girl
who can make music appear
at the touch of a button, Radio Girl
tunes into the waves of sound all around her,
zeroes in on a favorite channel, some far-off
neighbor with a voice like the moon, crooning
just above a whisper in their room, plucking
at lush guitar strings. Static breaks in—
someone's crying down the hall and the sobs
burst in staccato raindrops, then grease pops
in a skillet in the kitchen, and a mom sighs
to her friend on the line *I don't know*
where I've been the last five years of my life,
and, down the street, a percussion of knuckles
plays on the drumheads of growing bones,
there's the high-hat of laughter in a car clouded
with blunt smoke, a chorus of girls cracking up
in a circle, wailing sirens and newborns,
the nurse stuck in traffic after her shift,
pouring another day into another song,
praying it won't be long until she can finally
walk through her door.

In waves, our living fills her—music to her ears.
Alone as she is in this world, she doesn't have
to live in silence. She hears all the air between us,
how we scream in joy and fear.

Chapter Three

On a Pink Moon in April

I burn the book I just wrote.

I turn each page to smoke.

These stories needed me
to write them,
but I don't need them anymore.

There's a fine line
between facing the past
and staying stuck there,
so I send my attachment
to histories and memories
back to ashes and air.

I needed these words
to live in a book
so my body could let them go.

I'm obligated to complete the work,
but not to worry about
who does or doesn't read
or praise or loathe it,

because it set me free,
because I wrote it.

If You're Afraid of the Water

I don't blame you
or want to shame you.
Your fear is welcome here.

You're safe to be seen
facing your fear and flailing,
and I won't judge or turn away.

But if you want to spend one brave day
with me, I can wait patiently on the steps
of the pool, until you're ready.

I can hold you in my hands
as you float on your back and breathe
deep as the water lifts you.

I can teach you to swim the way
I teach frightened kids, the way my dad
taught me. *You don't have to hit*

the water, just open your arms to it,
gently, slowly. Move softly like the water,
and the water will move you.

We'll practice all day
until you trust your own limbs and the water
in the pool and the water in you moves together.

Or, if it's not in your nature to swim,
you can hold onto my shoulders,
and I'll carry you through the blue.

Origin Stories of a Soul

I'm the water's daughter.

My soul first swam on a lilac planet.
Abundance is everywhere,
money's not the only way to have it.

I wake up
to the thrum of cicadas and frogs down in the bog,
their thousand trilling voices melding into one song.

I came here to be good at my job, which is love.

I love humanity, that beautiful, awful experiment.
Animals who think and talk and dance like jungle birds
for our Gods, writing our history with war and bombs,
inventing new worlds with our symbols and speech,
our need to be loved and belong.

We're made of the same matter as a cat sleeping in the sun,
or a circle of trees, or a spattering of stars you can trace
into the shape of a woman collecting water from the river
in a jar.

My soul is as near as the ants building empires
among the grasses, as far as the most outstretched arm
of the Andromeda galaxy, as close as the blood-drumming
organ worn beneath my skin.

Each morning I rise to a new world being born.
When I greet the day, I say *I love you.*

I love you means *I want to watch you come alive.*

Our Oath to the Earth

for Becca & Fran
October 5th, 2019

When I push the seeds
   into their envelopes of dirt,
      I am telling the earth *I love you.*
When I water the flowering vines
   at the crest of the hill,
      I am telling the sky *I love you.*
When I place my hands on the trunk
   of the great grandmother oak
      & cast a spell for sunshine
in our lives, I am asking the world
   to hold a mirror to our light.

Before our wedding day, we've already
   taken this oath, to source our love
      for each other from this generous earth.
We've vowed
   if we're lucky enough to love a place,
      we will leave it
wild & abundant.
   May we leave it kinder
      & filled with more flowers
than when we found it.

May our love become a field
      of goldenrod & ironweed
where little homes can be built
   out of laughter & honest effort,
      & the labor of many hands
makes light work.

Teaching You the Moon

for a student

Your stories are a constellation of points
that often point nowhere or everywhere at once,
dear livewire, excessive talker,
endlessly enthusiastic one.
When it's story time in our basement classroom,
you're our shining star,
shuttling us from your dog's new sweater

to the white stuff in your uncle's car,
the police at the park,
you, alive, in your mom's tummy.
She was in jail and you both were so hungry.

Your tale ends in the present tense,
as you present the lunchbox
she's packed for you, brimming
with snacks, telling us about
your pink dollhouse,
where the plastic people you love
are always running
into walls and falling over.

Don't give up the glow of your own life
and its unhinged happenings,
dear student of show-and-tell,
is what I want to tell you.
Take these words and make them yours.
Take the past that tried to kill you
and turn today into a myth.

Before I share any of this,
you rise from your seat
and speak
of your Papa.

When the moon is a circle
that's when I see him,
and I can tell him I love him.

A different day, you'll say he was shot
on his front porch, planted flowers
in the backyard, read you books
in the crook of his arms.

My bosses all say you're lagging behind
in every goal you need to achieve
their charter school dream of *getting you*
to and through the mountain of college,
but some hours in the afternoon,
I want to sit and listen to you
tell of the mountains you've already marched,
because I know you'd never need me
to teach you the meaning of the moon.

You learned it on your own,

to search the sky for what's been stolen,
to reach for that glowing, lonely body
spinning in space above us,
to turn toward that cold rock
and name it love.

Radio Girl Glows

Her superpower is shining
a light on the dimmest places.
Nothing escapes the beam

of her smile. She once knocked out
a man with his hand raised
to crack the skull of his sad, old dog.
The waves rippling

from her radiant teeth
brought the man
to his knees, the dog thumping
its tail in the electric yellow puddle.

She helps girls find their way home
in the darkness, burns streetlights
brighter, blurs through the night
ahead of them, leaving a trail of
phosphorescence. There are plenty
of townspeople who are happy

she's here, but everyone knows
not to touch her.

Little Dancer

Danea dances on the playground
where every child is said to have a disability

but we are all able to do many things,
and Danea can dance like the whole

world is cheering her on.
With school lunches still bubbling

in our bellies, the sun scattering
its shine among the maples, Danea bolts

like a colt toward me, squeezes my knees,
and gives me a hug, pure sweetness.

She goes in a circle where all the aides
stand scanning the slides and swings,

head-counting each kid in their pack to be sure
no one's jumped the fence or stripped naked,

and she hugs each of us once. Then, she
tumbles into the ring and starts dancing,

squatting low, knees popping her up
like a firework, smiling with all her limbs.

We cheer her on, *Go Danea, Go* and
her movements grow into the most joyful

moment of my day. Her teacher
rushes forward, scolding her like a dog

who couldn't hold it in, *No, stop that, little girls*

don't dance like that!

She sends her away, puts her back in her place
and her body

with its skipped chromosomes and swollen
joints and breathing tube in her throat,

her body that we teach to sit still in a chair,
to stand in line, to be quiet, to be good.

Danea's teacher fumes at us, *Isn't it provocative,
isn't it troubling, it makes you wonder*

what she's watching at home. I find it troubling
we're playground-policing a young girl's dancing. Why?

Because dancing shows she has a body,
because she knows how to generate

a movement inside it? Because it shows a force
inside her soul we can't control?

I'm back with all the times I was told
to fold inside myself, draw tighter lines

around the noise and rhythm I longed to make.
I'd rather witness Danea dance all recess than listen

to anything this straight-and-narrow woman has to say.
The next day, when the little dancer hugs me, I tell her

what I need to hear myself,
Your joy is never too much.

Your joy is never too much.

Style & Fashion for People Who Don't Leave the House

Ballgown the bedsheets. Catwalk the sweatpants.
Dress your depression up in your finest fits.
Wear high heels and lipstick like you're pitching
the Universe your dream position
as you wash the piled-up dishes.

An hour you would've spent staring into screens,
stone-eyed, scrolling,
you can spend annointing yourself in cream and dust,
because make-up isn't just concealer
but what you reveal to yourself
the longer you paint your own gaze.

When there is nowhere left to go,
your body welcomes you home
with all your under eye baggage,
all the softness still here to celebrate
in your lips and hips.

If you can scavenge
some smoke and shadow and fabric,
you can make magic. Adorn the walls,
dress up your bones,
twirl in your skirts for no one.

Just kidding.
Aren't you someone?

Twirl in your skirts for no one but yourself,
the way even lifeless planets dance
in circles around the sun.

Aunt Sarah's Picture Is in Missouri Game & Fish

She's in high heels and a string bikini,
a bluegill dangling from her hook,
its scales like sequins that glitter in the sun.
The glossy caption reads,
Anyone can fish.

Aunt Sarah can do anything in high heels,
would've been a better caption.
She can balance in strappy black pumps
as she lugs a cooler, sloshing ice and beer
down the slanted gravel path, loading the van herself,
prepping us for a float trip where she teaches me
all I need to know at fourteen: how to be a woman
on the river, how to stake your own tent,
how to light a fire, how to handle
the gaggle of women in floppy hats,
faces slathered in sunscreen,
loudly making fun of her outfit.
Aunt Sarah goes right up to them and says, not unkindly,
Ladies please, I'm trying to show my niece all the ways
she's unstoppable, and your example teaches her the opposite.

When I turn this poem into my professor,
he strikes out a few lines and writes a single note,
Great "woman-poem."

Missed the mark again.
This isn't a song about empowered women,
but an ode to the way we erode other people's perceptions
when we listen to the force inside our own bodies,
a force like the river, which try as we might to dam
and control it, always barrels home to the ocean,
always flows toward the true source of power.

When I swim in the river, I am so much like Sarah.
I tuck my head under and throw my weight against the current,
swimming upstream, surging with my strength
even though the river is much stronger,
and I'm connected, not to what is expected of me,
but to the stream alive inside my body, reminding
none of us live forever, while some have so much to give,
looks to serve and heads to turn and trails to blaze
as the relentless water moves on.

The Waitress Sucks It Up

The vacuum inhales the broken bodies
of breadcrumbs, and my body
exhales another full day done
as I dance through the diner, sucking up
the mess of Sunday's rush,
the husks of food disappearing
in a snapping, static *woosh*.

The door chimes and a herd of men
stumble in, leathered and liquored,
past the sign that we close in ten minutes.
I bring them the red plastic basket
of re-heated rolls,
I poise my pen above my pad
and ask what they're having.

The last man wraps up his order,
cat-arches his back, fiddles his toothpick
between candy corn teeth, looks me up and down,
the motion in his eyes like a fork and a knife,
and asks if I'm *on the menu,*
and *can they see me naked?*

I could've spit out something so simple.
Fuck you. Do you know who you're talking to?
Excuse me, rude. But after nine hours of fake smiles
and running through the customer service script,
I reach for my own voice and come up empty.

I turn on my heels and storm to the kitchen,
my anger catching on the vacuum cord,
ripping it from the wall. Another man laughs,
Look, you almost made her fall over her own feet.

I don't spit in their food. I don't dip their cups

in the bucket of bleach. Instead
I do all I've been trained to,
stacking seven plates along my arms,
so it will only take one trip, another waitress
removing the plates while I stand still as a statue,
telling her who ordered what.

Having saved his dish for last, I place it before him myself.
I rip off
the check and say I don't have time
for their disrespect,
so they can take care of themselves.

I plug the vacuum back into the wall and bask
in its high-whine roar.
I don't need to show them the giant
I know that I am. I float on
as entire towns of breadcrumbs
vanish in my path.

Universe, Give Claire the Keys to the Garden

Give my girl a plot of earth for her office. Give her a school
of unruly ranunculus and daffodils for children.
Let the next generation grow up beneath her steady hand.

Universe, let a woman working among women celebrate you
with flowers, with their soft science, their tender lifespans
and voluminous stores of sun.

I want my friends to find what fills them, I want them to be
an instant yes at every interview. My wish: they're given
whatever set of keys they need.
Keys to libraries, film sets, supply closets filled
with rare paints, a seed catalogue.

Universe, set my friends in the fields where their work
will flourish. Sync their sleep with the timetable ticking deep
within the earth. Pluck them from their beds, hold their clean-
cut stalks to the sun and nudge them into new territory.

Let them uproot as many times as it takes to claim their calling.
Let the transplantation feel like coming home.

The Sirens of Rainbow Basin Creek

Don't think of us as seductresses,
when it's the creek who seduces us.

We're not here to shipwreck a sailor
or steal your married man, okay?

But when it's the first May day
that rings with summer heat,
and the spring-fed creek sings
clear water tunes, her music babbling
over stones and roots, her ice-melt
whirlpooling in the dappled sun,
why on Daddy God's Green Earth
would these witches keep their clothes on?

If by chance a hunter or hiker spies us
slipping panties off our ankles in the sun,
painting each other's faces with clay and mud,
braiding smooth blue aster blooms
into each other's hair, building cairns
of silt and pebbles on our nipples,
we're not to blame if they fall in love.

We only came here to play,
not to be watched,
after getting our messages direct
from the pollen-gods, those dust motes
of sex fuzz floating among the trees,
but then a twig snaps under the thud of boots,
and we snap faster than lightning
back into our bras and denim and tees.
Lickety-split, we transform from creek sirens
into college kids, back from mythical creatures
into women who don't want any trouble

or to get murdered in the woods.

By the time we're dressed
and hiking home,
sunlight stinging our cheeks,
sand in our shoes,
eyes flicking over our shoulders,
eyes wide at the trail ahead,

we're sure of who we've always been,

women creating magical realms
in the company of other women.

Radio Girl *Is* Like Other Girls

Possessing the powers of
super-seeing, super-hearing,
super-being doesn't mean
you're super popular.

Radio Girl doesn't need to be seen as different,
but when you've got a green glow
and a visible aura of electromagnetic energy
trailing everywhere you go,
when you've got spores in your skin that eat
through trash and plastic, when you've got
radio antennas that pull music and sound
from the clouds embedded in your fingertips,
folks get to talking about how you think
you're special, getting too big for your britches.

Radio Girl understands the enormity
of her would-be mission. If she'd just take up the cause
she could travel the earth cleaning up mortals' messes
before humanity causes their own destruction.

But she craves Friday nights at the movies
with a gaggle of girls, buttered popcorn
with chocolate candies mixed in.
She wants to learn French braids and French kissing.
Skip school to eat French fries and get high
behind the dumpster.

Radio Girl grew up in a radioactive dump
in the Murder Capital of the #1 Meth State,
and maybe she just wants to be French, okay?

But every time she tries to get close
to the other girls they call her *alien* and *freak*.

Maybe they're afraid Radio Girl will think
them plain and ordinary, without radiation-fueled
superpowers of their own, so they hurl the first stone
before they have a chance to get hurt.

But Radio Girl thinks other girls are magic
and she's drawn to all they have in common
as much as their messy opposites.

If there's anything she shares with the other girls,
the neighborhood children, the women, men, people,
the earthly brethren, the possums and trash cats
and chained-up dogs,
it's that she'll grow
as strong as she needs to,
as soft as she must.

The Waitress Takes Feet Pics

She knows she'll never show them,
never sell them or make her millions
with photos of lotioned heels and French-tipped nails,
when her feet look less like a fetish
and more like an ogre's.

But she loves these tattered, calloused things,
these wings below her ankles, blisters blooming
inside each other like tree rings,
so she takes a picture for herself.

She marvels at the swollen pads of skin,
the blueprint for bunions she inherited
from her grandma, who foregoes surgery and walks
with a limp. Notices her pinky toes curling
toward the others like the shyest little sister.

When she was twelve and learning
to see her own body, she said out loud,
My feet are ugly.
Her dad snapped back,
Well at least you have a pretty face.
Would you rather have an ugly face
but pretty feet?

Thanks Dad, she thinks, the memory resurfacing
as she soothes coconut oil into her soles after her shift.
Thank you for the reminder
that if prettiness makes people comfortable,
then ugliness keeps the world in motion,
so beauty must be where the body goes to feel whole.

When she feeds and waters the streaming crowds,
her face is a flower, growing toward the light

she sees in everyone. When she walks two miles home
after eight hours of ache, the arches of her feet split
at the seams, a teddy bear's stuffing spooling out.

In passing, some people tell her
she's got a good head on her shoulders,
but it's her head that gives her all the trouble.

She knows what's she got
and it's two feet firm on the ground,
a web of roots that drink from the dirt
and grip the earth,
holding her high and proud.

There's No Marriage in Heaven, But There Is Love

I don't want to marry one person
and expect them to bring me heaven.

I love the thrill of falling in love
with myself through someone else's eyes,

so I'm safer with seven husbands, seven
wives, a soulmate every season.

I see no reason for being someone's *one and only*
when I could be one among many.

The love I want is more than a family
and less than a country—

call it a culture, a village, a club, a cult.
I used to call it a café where I worked

and spent my days feeding people, reading
people, and my job was essential to the steady thrum

of money-music streaming through our neighborhood.
The baristas played each other's playlists on the speakers,

and with unified tunes, we coordinated in a kitchen
the size of a shoebox, and flowed through coffee-river rushes

as the morning poured into afternoon.
I fall in love with places pouring people

into a rhythm, a litany of rituals, a drumming circle,
a field where our children run, one giggling herd of cousins.

After a year of being touch-starved, I only want to sleep
in a puddle of people I love beneath the stars.

We'll put ourselves to bed like babies with our bottles
of bubbles, we'll laugh and deep dive our way past midnight

into the light of a new day, and in the morning
we'll thank the dull ache behind our eyes

as we rise to clean up the trash and glass we left behind.

Ten Inches

Schools all over St. Louis began closing early,
the sky dumping buckets of white fluff all over
the roads. I clocked out on a Friday, a spring
in my step, because I was a tired, underpaid teacher
& the weekend ahead demanded only rest &
nestling into thick blankets & chocolate melted
to sludge. The other last-minute grocery store goers
& I were a hive of mayhem, Aldi picked clean
of greens & loaves of bread. Like schoolchildren,
we waited before the milk & eggs & juice in a line.

A kind woman & I ushered each other to go next,
Go ahead, no you. She said, *I'm just getting orange juice.*
Me too, I said, *what kind,* & when she said whichever one,
I grabbed two of my usual & handed her the other.
We can become so generous when we know we'll be
locked away from the world in our shelters, everyone
telling everyone, *be safe.* We can be so angry on the road:
shouting matches, hydroplaning death traps, everyone
secretly breaking down inside their cars. I barely made it
up the hill, but you were there, waiting on our porch,
carried bags in the crook of your arm, drew me close.
In the bath, I drank too much cheap red wine & stewed
until I was all bleeding heart, all prune. You cooked
the sausage & I made the chili, draining vino & telling
you stories about how wild I'd been at fifteen, eighteen,
sneaking into clubs, grinding in trains of ladies ten deep,
busting condoms on early a.m. playgrounds. *Drink more,*
you said, in awe of who I become when I'm freed, *I need
more stories.* The next story was born between our bodies

& we blew through the rooms, tumbling out the front door,
the quiet night illuminated by inches & inches of ice.
You laid down sleeping bags & blankets, & in the dry stripe

beneath the overhang we joined at the hips & lips, warm liquid
passing between us, the sky cracking its jaw inside us, so when
your body shot a flurry of drift inside me, your eyes rolling
into your head, I was like tree sap, wet & weepy, thinking
Oh my God, they're pure as snow.

We Fell in Love at Shit Lake

It was our first date. I said I knew a place.

We'd been drinking like fish
the night before but couldn't hear each other
over the buzzing hive of the bar,
so I didn't know much about you,
until I led us through the rugged jungle
to the edge of the lake. You went right for it,
holding your beer overhead as you stumbled in,
wading in your jorts, which is when I knew you
were the kind of person who would cut
a pair of jeans above the knee
to give them a second life, the kind who would fray
and grow softer, a truer blue with age.

You were up to your navel in the lake,
not the aquamarine sheen of tourism posters,
but water the color of trees and salt and fields of grain
and I trusted you wouldn't flinch when I said,

So I used to be in love with this lake,
and then I found out it was full of shit,
but even that didn't stop me
from being in love with it.
I did some reading.
It's not as bad as they make it sound,
so it's safe to swim here.
As long as there's no outbreak.

You didn't bat an eye.
Just sipped your beer and replied,
in your voice of brass and burning rubber,
the voice of a man who's waded through
a hundred-year-flood in knee-high muck boots,

Well, every lake is full of shit.
Can't let that stop you from swimming.

It's been five years since, and the water keeps rising,
as does this abundant flood of fucked up mess,
but we paddle, we float, we hold each other
and bob together with our breaths.
The water hasn't stopped us yet.

Before I Let It Go

I stew in it. I brew a cup of coffee
and ruminate with it. I think to call my friends
to bitch about it, but I feel like bitching less and less.
Before giving it up, I give it one final round of edits
seventy-seven more times. One more try. Before surrender,
I clench. *My pain, my pleasure, my bliss, my grief.*
I can't let go of this: it's me. Prior to release,
I squeeze and wring my fingers, crack all my knuckles, tiny
explosions of bubbles bursting between my bones. Before I let go,
I hold tight. To all I love, to my life. Eventually I remember
none of it was solely mine. Then, I fall in love with all my debt,
this endless expense of borrowed time.

Radio Girl Leaves Town

The radioactivity which makes her extraordinary
is slowly killing the people around her.
She didn't ask for that kind of power,
and she doesn't want to milk it
to rake in the dollars. She turns down a deal
with Marvel after they pitch her a script
where the villain is named *Shadow Man*
instead of the Military-Industrial Complex.
When the nation finally pays attention
to the contamination in North County, St. Louis,
every news outlet wants to interview her,
not the children and elders dying of rare cancers,
not their caretakers. At first, the cameras feel
like the attention she never had as a child,
but then they just feel like more hungry mouths,
mouths that call her miracle, spectacle, hoax.
She's hounded by scientists asking to study
her anatomy, podcasters asking to pick her brain.
Their questions all sound the same.
When did you know you had this power?
No one asks about the years of souring garbage
or the songs she sang in a castle made
of cardboard. She craves a return to her roots,
a depth at which no one knew her.
She leaves town without plan of returning,
but even a radioactive teen girl can't predict the future.
This walk into the woods is the gesture
of a woman who longs to know herself,
who believes the deep, dark miles have magic
to teach her. She sprints on without the weight
of the people who never needed her
to save them in the first place.

The Water Is Not a Dead Girl

is not her blue rotting body
birthed from the lake at dawn

is not the team of divers
midwives in scuba gear
and rubber masks
pulling her from the canal
a stillborn

the water is not a girl
who goes missing
who no one looks for

is not the cold porcelain bowl
where the toilet water ripples
with the splash of guts and bile
as a girl who wishes to vanish
probes the flat end of a toothbrush
down her neck's soft tunnel

is not the plastic
is not the poison
is not the islands of trash in the ocean

is not the bloated fish
oil-slicked bellies spoiling in the sun

the water is not what we've done
to the water is not
the depths we fill with our waste
the truth we won't face the water

remembers eternity

is both a solitary force

and a living collection
of twenty septillion drops

and the water molecules?
are like old sisters

they've been everywhere together

and when it rains they bump into each other
they laugh at how long it's been

how no matter how hard
the world tries

their souls are ancient
and they will not die

after Lucille Clifton
thank you

Radio Girl Doesn't Know It Yet

But there's a girl in Chernobyl
teaching herself to fly.

There's a girl in Flint
learning how to turn
leady water
into rivers of blood
and wine

and a boy on the island of Tuvalu
who's training to raise
underwater mountains
from rising ocean tides.

All over the earth,
young giants are waking up.
Ancient spirits are being called forth.

The past is barreling us
into a future we won't recognize at all.
The lone girl walks on.

Radio Girl first found freedom
in the sentence
I am my own best friend.

She's right.

And there is so much she doesn't know yet.

For the Old Woman I Dream of Being

Let me go silver.
Let my skin go soft as spun silk.
Let the water in my eyes go milk.

May the Milky Way spray across my shoulders
in a constellation of sunspots.

Let me outlast every broadcast of apocalypse.
Let me outlive the days of doom and the looming end.

Let me be a grandma, a matriarch, a bad bitch.

I know this is a selfish wish
when right now so many people pray for just one more day,
to see their face one final time.

What good is a greed like mine?

I'm not sure, but today I need strength
so I imagine myself an elder with silver rivers to my waist
tending to my garden, whether among ruins or riches,
as long as there is a patch of dirt and grass,
I will grow marigolds and keep chickens.

Let me slick my raisin-wrinkled lips
with drug store lipstick
the color of crushed grapes.

Let me keep my teeth in a jar of water,
polish them on my sleeve,
slip them in my gums,
sink my fangs into a bursting peach.

I was raised up to think if a woman was touched

by the presence of beauty,
her beauty would wither in decades.

And if a woman was touched by the presence
of brilliance, we would only remember her
if she was a tragedy.

So I thought dying young and full of flame
was the way to go.

Then it seemed the Earth herself was a tragic woman,
always on the brink of some self-shattering disaster,
and I wanted desperately to live a long, ripe life
so I could care for her and my people in their twilight hours,

which is when I stopped looking at myself
through the camera of a culture
that would never love me
for my naked, animal self,

and I began to live for the quiet, solitary truth of my body,
my factory of overworked and underpaid cells laboring
to keep me alive and well in a world that feeds itself
a steady diet of sickness and misery.

For no other reason than how lovely it sounds,
let me lounge all day in a long linen nightgown,
listening to all the records left behind
by the stars who blazed the charts
and burned up by twenty-seven.

Let me know the names of all the birds on my block by their song.
Let me live until music becomes
my final language, my mother tongue.

When the music runs out, cover me in dirt
and plant a tree in my heart. Let the roots drain me dry.
Let the earth drink me up.

Notes

pg. 48

In the opening line of "The Only Girl in a Car Full of Boys"
I borrow from the poem "What Did I Love" by Ellen Bass.

pg. 90

The title for "There's No Marriage in Heaven But There Is Love"
is a line from "Sarah Brown" in *Spoon River Anthology* by Edgar
Lee Masters.

pg. 91-92

"The Water Is Not a Dead Girl" is after Lucille Clifton's "the earth
is a living thing."

Acknowledgements

I'm indebted to the work of Karen Nickel and Dawn Chapman of Just Moms STL for my knowledge of the radioactive waste legacy in North County, St. Louis. Thank you to Rebecca Cammisa, the director of *Atomic Homefront,* and her entire team for unearthing these long-buried stories in my hometown.

Many thanks to my editor, Kallie Falandays, for embracing the wildness at the heart of this book and helping these poems sing. Thank you to Miranda Lorikeet for your gorgeous art of women, water, and isolation.

Thank you to the faculty, staff, and students of Pacific University for creating such a generous, engaging writing community. A special thanks to Kwame Dawes, Ellen Bass, Mahtem Shiferraw, and Joseph Millar for their guidance and clear vision as I shaped these poems.

Thank you to UrbArts and MK Stallings for all you do to give young poets in St. Louis a platform. I'm so grateful to every poet who has raised the stakes of poetry on the Urb stage.

To the girls and women I grew up with and have grown alongside—y'all deserve the world. I'm always rooting for you. This book is for you.

To my family, there aren't enough words of gratitude. Thank you for the love and support and creative freedom you've always given me. Thank you for all the intergenerational curses you broke so I could grow up knowing and believing in my own wholeness. And to the village of women that raised me, the long lineage of single mothers and resilient spirits I come from, I will always carry you in my heart.

Thank you to my stubborn self for finishing this book during a pandemic, global uprisings against racial injustice, and a year of so much collective grief. There were days when writing felt impossible, so I'm grateful to every artist and storyteller who has continued to show up.

Chris, there is a thank you written into every one of these pages with your name on it. Your steadiness and support have carried me through my first book and so much else. I love you.